THE DISORDER OF LOVE

karen connelly

Gutter Press   Toronto · New York

Gutter Press acknowledges the support received for its
publishing program from the Canada Council's Project
Grant Program.

Canadian Cataloguing in Publication Data

Connelly, Karen, 1969-
  The disorder of love
A Caroline Lonsdale Book
Poems
ISBN 1-896356-11-7

I. Title.
PS8555.O546D57 1997   C811'.54   C97-930425-3
PR9199.3.C66D57 1997

Published by Gutter Press, 118 Peter Street, suite 1,
Toronto, Ontario, Canada M5V 2G7
http://www.salzmann.com/gutter
Represented in Canada by the Literary Press Group
Distributed in Canada by General Publishing,
30 Lesmill Rd, Don Mills, Ontario
Distributed in the U.S. by D.A.P.
Distributed Art Publishers, Inc.
155 Avenue of the Americas, 2nd Floor,
New York, NY 10013-1507
(Tel 212.627 1999 Fax 212.627 9484).
To order, call 1 800 338 BOOK

Manufactured in Canada

ACKNOWLEDGEMENTS

Many of these poems have appeared or will appear in the following journals: *Arc, Descant, Dandelion, Event, Fiddlehead, The New Quarterly, Room of One's Own, Poetry Canada, Pottersfield Portfolio, Salt* (Australia), *Island* (Australia), *Stand* (England).

I thank Nancy Holmes, for her work with the manuscript and for her love. I thank Libby Oughton, an inspiring, remarkable friend. I would also like to acknowledge the University of New Brunswick English Department for my 1992-93 residency, during which time I worked on many of these poems. The various subjects in my photographs and poems also have my deep appreciation, especially Antigone, Venetia, Yiorgos, Amalia, Voula and Andreas; Psinia herself made the Greek poems possible. Towards my mother Jackie Henry, I feel more gratitude than I am capable of describing or ever repaying.

FOR NANCY HOLMES AND ALEXANDRA KEIM

Great love is always the result
of a past mistake.

Leo Tolstoy, from Anna Karenin

THE DISORDER OF LOVE

Table of Contents

THE ORDER EPHEMEROPTERA

The Disorder of Love

Chaos is a Greek Word

The Order Ephemeroptera

*...desire perishes
because it tries to be love.*

Jack Gilbert

Riderless

Times ago, I heard your voice
   drifting down the river
   and this journey began.

At night I am coming
towards you, loping
easily over the land.
Sweat chills my face and back.
I will run riderless like this until I find you.

From the last hard tongue of tundra
   to the forests
   where wolves hide in curtains of snow

   I have been searching for you

   past foxes and weasels who swivel
   their chiselled skulls to watch me run.

From the forests to the fields
   where the owls bear down
   like blizzard-winged phantoms
Through the foothills chanting higher and higher,
   watch how the mountains surround me,
     rise at my naked flanks like white-hooded monks
       hungry for the moon.

The moon is a mouth spilling opal
but I don't want her.
Her body is cold and her heart is a bone.
She never bleeds and she cannot sing.

At night I am coming towards you.
When I find you we will not be lost.
It does not matter how far you've wandered.
I will bring you back with me,
show you the sun-drinking fields, the forests,
the rapids where I swam my mad ballets.
The mountains in daylight will be cathedrals
of stone and pine and soprano wind.

There I will lay open the supple earth of my body,
    this hot plain breathing from breast to belly.

I will give you this, my own wild acre of Brazil.

THE INNOCENCE OF DOORS

Across the hall, his guests
    are keeping me awake.
He leaves his doors open, always.
The people laugh hard as whisky melts
    their throats, oils their eyes.
Their whispers are the size of ospreys.

I have heard this before, in another house.
Once I lived near the ocean,
    where the people slept in vaults of gold light
    and woke humming to dance at night, their fingers
        strumming skin.

I told them
    Leave me alone
    Don't sing
    Stop singing!

    Their voices tangled the air.
        They looped me in and gave me a black-eyed centaur.
        I learned to live naked there.

Now I live in a rocky place
    and breathe ice-wind.
My awkward hands cradle stone.
I wear wool.

But the voices across the hall
    are green frogs laughing,
    leaping from one tongue to another.
The man who lives in that room
    makes love to the wind and opens
    his doors to the moon-washed sky.

All day I write.
At night, I want human letters.
I want him to braid his songs into my hair.

But what curious kisses could I whisper in his ear?
My tongue is dipped deep blue in ink.
My hands sink through a quicksand of words.

Close these eyes.
Touch my lips and stretch my body smooth
     in the bed of their naked laughter.
I fall asleep to the sound
     of voices across the hall, opening,
          glowing throats beyond the wall.

How long can we live with these doors so open?

THE LESSER AMAZON

Last night I dreamt
I was the salamander
who does not burn in fire:
I swallowed saffron tongues of flame.

In South America, tree frogs live
in the pooled water of bell-shaped leaves.
They never touch earth but make their choir
in a ripe canopy, serenading higher
than the skulls of hunters.

Those very frogs leap from my rhododendron
into the kitchen sink.
Shreds of jungle dazzle the old house.
Where are all these vines growing from?
This morning a parrot torpedoed over the table.
Yesterday afternoon in the bathtub,
after a surge of curious hissing,
I found a nest of baby snakes beneath
the bathmat, living red leather,
tongues flicking an ancient orange.
They covered my feet in an exotic reptile weave,
wound up my shins, looped themselves
around my waist and neck, slid anxiously
through my slick hair.
It took me an hour to comb them out
and send them slithering to the garden.

It can't go on like this.
The neighbours gossip:
    Has she seduced baboons?
    Is she making love to panthers?
Birds of paradise have chased away the sparrows
and the problem with peacocks
is the potency of their screams.

Creatures peer from the trees
of these turquoise nights, listening
to me rush through the rainforest of my body,
searching for you.

Deep into cardinal soil I plunge my hands,
praying to plant you in this jungle.

Love, my throat is the lesser Amazon.
I want you to slide in.

Carve a slim-ribbed canoe.
Learn how to swim.

THE PURE ANIMAL

Now do you see, now
do you feel them?

Watch the animals waken around us,
inside, see these creatures pant
and pace through their paintings,
anxious to escape the canvas, eager
to prowl in the night garden
of this house.

Don't fear them, you're animal yourself,
these heights are ours, these subterranean caves.
Don't be afraid of the depths,
drowning, let your body drop
through this bed, a cream ocean, feel
the undertow of twisted sheets,
the waves of feather and fin.

I throw my limbs up like ropes
to haul you in, the mane of your hair
falls down, wind and scent rise
from your neck like the earth
where you have run.

No metaphor is wet enough,
no metaphor is right,
these words never touch
    the skin and teeth, never feed
    the starving arms, never loosen
    these legs that long to gallop
        down the night.

You rear up like a horse
    (my arms the ropes that rein you in)
      your blood vaults through
        the meadow of your skin

  and just seeing you waken, rise like that,
    just seeing you shudder
      floods me, the inland sea, the inlet
        the in, in, in

When you give me yours, take mine,
fruit cleaves from the stone,
our sinews twist cobra from our bones

The animals around us waken.
The animals in us rise wild.

This is everything, we make this, love,
    this is us, the panther in the museum
      when it springs from the canvas
        in a precise torrent of black and gold,
        crimson paw prints on the polished floor,
        all the doors broken open

THE CHEAT

The sky unbraids her oyster-blue hair,
hurls rough pearls of hail at my skin.
One man flees over the flesh
of a continent surging in spring.

The other man is here, the man I crush
like the mad one who slams the door shut
on her lover's fingers, who cannot stop
slamming the door, cannot stop.
He cries now in the small room.
He opens a plate glass window with his fist
and walks into the rain.
He will wander this city for hours,
wearing my old coat.

I cannot wear it myself now.
The nerves of his pain still spark
and snap inside it.
Fury clings like a gargoyle
to the shoulders,
the long sleeves,
the rain-whipped back.
The man feeds this gargoyle
like he once fed me, a famished lover.

Once I thought I knew my heart, that red
kestrel soaring in such a shallow sky.
Now I can't see it, I don't know where it is.
I find vultures cleaning their beaks on my ribs.

After sins luxurious, mundane,
count the faces cut with sorrow.

What can I do with so much pain?
There is no suitcase big enough for it,
no abyss deep enough to bury it,
no incinerator for the burning eye and heart.
We tether the shreds of ourselves together
and cry it, cry it, cry it,
until the bed is soaked,
and hemlock sprouts delicate lime
from the sweaty folds of the sheets.
He whispers, *Your body sowed this poison.*

ONE MORE WOMAN BEGS TO
COMPLETE HER LOVER

Once upon a time
they twined tight
round the spool in my gut,
but now the songs unravel in the singing.
Words knot around the table legs,
the arms of chairs, our wrists.
Words spin down to the bed
like maple keys that will never
open the earth.

Oh Joseph.
I've torn a hole in the sky.
Fly through.

Why do you turn away
to watch the small yellow bird
dance and chatter in his kingdom of weeds?
Why do you wring your hands like unclean rags
after steeping them in my hot gloss?

I am an open door.
Walk away after entering but
    step through me.

Come across this threshold—

This Dumb Melodrama

I leave you on the highway beside a cemetery.
Crooked headstone teeth grin and leer.
Farther up, road-kill gives a feast to the ravens.

Christ, to get fed
so simply.
Enough poetry.
I'm sick of it,
    Whitman and the elegies,
        the oatmeal and apples in your pack.
The wind plucks a senseless tune
on your shrouded guitar.

I push you from the borrowed car,
kiss the mouth you've lent me these months.
Hurry, hurry, go now,
cut your poetic tongue
out of my mouth.

I leave you by a field of green wheat.
Grasshoppers razor blind against the wind,
strike your wrists, the book in your hand.

*   *

I drove away howling love
in perfect time with wind
thrashing hair in my eyes.
A wasp died skewered on sunlight
against the back window.
You caught a ride east.

I am learning
the list of what I do not own.

Least of all, I do not own those roads you travel now,
the steel arteries of this country
pumping petrol blood, the earth's muscles
torn open and beaten black with ashphalt.
I do not own the spring-born mud.
The fierce engines roar on without me.

I untie myself from the tracks
of this dumb melodrama.
Stand up filthy, covered
in dust and pigeon shit,
a fool, a fool.

But I stay here.
I will not follow
fear, your one-eyed
highway, your backward
migration.

THERE ARE CHARMS FOR EVERY KIND OF JOURNEY

A bird I've never seen threads a desolate song
through this labyrinth of pines.
Dusk comes, then the indigo oil of night.
Mountains dive and rise like dolphins.
Tonight I will dream of the Bay of Biscay,
the shores where I will breathe without you.
You cannot sleep by the sea.

If you were still here, I would whisper,
   Lay your hand on my back.
   This moment is all.
   There will be no more.

Train whistles pierce every black hour,
wise arrows in this witless heart.
The engines cry, Come away   come away.

You once said, It's hard to lie in the mountains.
Then you lied beautifully, without blinking.
We are not clean enough to live here.

You left weeks ago,
I leave tomorrow at dawn.
Simplicity is the birthright of deer
who do not name days or plan betrayals.
My life is a broken bridle
and yours is an antique clock.

I wanted to give you a talisman
whose loss wouldn't maim me.
There are charms for every kind of journey.
You needed an owl's black claw,
or a scorpion imprisoned in amber
or my anklebone.

The trains in this deaf country
don't hold people anymore
but I'm going to find one
to drag my heart away from this valley.

I need a train.
I need that kind of weight and roar
to rip your gentle lyrics out of my mouth.

Dear Joseph

Late afternoon, it's raining.
This is the only letter I will not send.
We've axed the noble goodbyes, the relentless jokes.
I must do this, you said, *I regret nothing.*
You suck your vision of wholeness
like a boy sucking a tarnished penny.

You are so rich.

You are not here, old lover.
Someone else already sleeps in sheets
I've not yet washed.
I mourned for a month.
Disgusting, isn't it,
the hip bones gnashing
in that creaky bed.

Even this beautiful house, we've beaten.
Boxes, torn books and letters, crumbling roses
litter the hallway and living room.
Two large moths, soul-mates, have died
and dried in my tea pot.
I rub the powder of their failed flights
between my fingers.

I trip over books on the floor
to find the pen which scribbles this
last note to you, my own true heart

my own true heart because you told me,
Understand: I do not love well.

I sit in a cream slip, dirty hair uncombed.
If I were willow-boned, Blanche and I
could be sisters, the setting is perfect,
the torn dress in the closet,
the gas stove, the guilty bottle.
But not me, I'm no weeping willow,
my shoulders are too broad,
my accent northern.

Rain crashing there, past my neck, on the window,
as a spider unfolds over the sill, hooking
eight hair-thin limbs over the African violet.
On the stereo, the Russian composer
gifts Scheherezade with a voice again,
sets her pirouetting from one stunning story to another.

The king begins to adore her mouth,
the way she licks her lips, inhales so quickly...
He sees her splendid teeth are ivory and knows
he can never kill her, she must live on
with him, he loves her silken see-through words.

But this is hardly Arabia
and I was never a virgin princess.
My clothes are wrinkled and practical.

My underwear dry out their loneliness
in the bathroom.

I let the plants die.

Autumn comes early.

Who loves well?

TEMPORARILY

The details of your face
escape like minnows.
Don McKay

I abandon men,
temporarily,
and come to the cabin.
I sit on the porch mending
the messy tear in my left ventricle.
Night blues the lake,
sweeps the shore with raven-wing.
A moth beats an ash tattoo
against the lampshade.

Inside, the women play cards, drink,
and laugh with occasional hysteria.

I've spent a third of my life
listening to those sounds,
envisioning pillows, pliable
hand-warmed cards, assorted glasses.
I've learned to drink Scotch and beer,
negotiating entrance to those pools of talk.

It does not matter.
Human waters drain away from me.
The women in the other room howl.
They discuss an older woman's ugly hair.

Has anything on earth ever been so funny?

* *

Morning, I walk into the orchard
of apricot sky, crushing Venus's slippers
and shooting stars with glee.
I stop at the locoweed
like a starving cow and
eat, eat.
Later I slide the canoe out,
inhale the wide death of rivers.
I consider drowning.

Unfortunately, I am a strong swimmer,
it would take an alligator
or an Atlantic storm to haul me under.

Hours later, when I glide
fierce and burnt along the dock,
the expensive puppy barks,
shakes light from its pedigree fur.
The mistress of canoe and cabin
turns over on her towelly spit.
She yawns, extraordinarily
bored with her magazine, and asks

Did you have a nice time?
Isn't the lake lovely?
Aren't you afraid of the depth
out there?

* *

I sit in the shade for so long
my feet grow cold, though the heat
of high summer is a royal iguana, languid,
lording over the stones near the lake.

I no longer wait for Joseph.
On a phone his dead voice intoned,
Do not think of me as your lover

and I do not, I watch birds devouring moths instead
(vowing: I am no dull moth)

No, I do not think of him.
I disremember him.
I summon his naked reflection out of my mirror.

He is not my lover, I sing to myself, plucking
his finger-husks from the spiderweb above my bed.
I bait fish hooks with my own bitter grubs
and eat rainbow trout until my eyes feel blue.

I swim miles above star-rippled rocks.
No one knows, but the whole lake
is laden with opals and moonstones.
I walk alone on the dirt roads.
Trees lean over to touch my shoulders
like the lover I no longer have.

Oh, to sleep in those jade palaces of shade,
those alcazars of leaf and shadow.
Earth's emerald scent thrives inside me.
When I howl in a blown sea of wheat,
no one can tell my voice from the wind's.

*   *

The inhabitants of my life:

birds whose names I learn and forget

these flowers lying on the table
like faeries fast asleep

the disgruntled porcupine bristling under the moon,
snorting at me when I come out with a candle

that woman down there in the water, smiling,
talking philosophy, fashion, gin rummy.
She bobs on a styrofoam cloud.
Her hair unlike the ugly hair of old women,
she floats, with elegance, towards death.

*   *

And the child, I cannot forget
the neighbour's child,
whose eyes are scattered with fresh hay.
Sunset writes the lyrics of a girl's limbs
in blue water, her body
sheathed in green as she dives,
hands hungry for the pulse of stone.
Above her, long gold spoons stir the lake.

Pulling herself up on the dock,
she is the mermaid fool who surrendered her tail.
Her skin shivers beneath
the velvet curiosity of bees
who believe her dress is a garden.
Lace wings halo her knees,
copper threads shine in her drying hair.

I kiss her cool forehead.
She dances on the dock.

Ephemeroptera

In the beginning I was young, I whispered:
your words fill my body's well
your voice ripens stone
your words run the river emerald.
In the beginning I was very young.

We went to a lake.
The great pelicans flew
slowly, like exhausted angels.
At night the torrent of your fingers
made me pant
    Believe in this   Believe in this
though it was a lie.

Yes. Our bodies lied.
Your weight crashing down
like earth from a mountainside
had nothing to do with the truth.
A natural disaster, yes, but what
was I doing in the mountains anyway?

I scraped my ankle on the rocks
watching the most vivid rainbow
we had ever seen
but that, too, was a false sign.
I wish the cut had been deep enough
to leave a scar, I wanted
something to remember you by.

Nothing was true enough to stay.
Now I drag a stick through the gutter
of my memory, searching for leftovers.
The mayflies.
Miniature dragons fluttered around us
those days by the lake, clung
to the cabin screens, landed in our hair.
The order *ephemeroptera*.

Born without true mouths, they rise from water
only to mate, even food unnecessary
when clean biological lust is life.
Our naked feet crushed thousands on the roads.
Cheap tar and the seasonal carnage of mayflies
designed our soles, stuck to our heels.

Now lean over Joseph, look into the well.
Not your exquisite voice ringing there
but dead insects blinding the water's eye.

Do Not Dream Of These People Anymore

The vision of Maya turning
   in a crowded room, wordless,
      to embrace me.
    She was too slender, shoulders roped
      to her neck with green ribbon.
     Her husband sat on the edge of a chair,
      eyes like gouged clay,
      whispering, *I love her.*

Do not dream of these people anymore.
Like the dead, they inhabit severed countries.
They wake and sleep at different hours.
As you envision them, they might live
those exact movements
with other people,
but never with you.

You twist awake in a cold room
with too many windows.
Scarves and sheets curtain out the street.
Someone has given you irises.
Littered paper on the floor demands attention.
Shaquil has left a note saying he is broke,
will you lend him money?
In the narrow bed, a book suffocates
under your elbow.

Pour the people of the dream into a kettle,
boil them.
They evaporate.
Do they settle on your ceiling?
Or do you drink them with your coffee?

37

Because night after night, they rise
    from you anew, explaining themselves,
        furious, and he makes love to you again,
            and again she cries,
                and Gabriel cuts up
                    photographs and old snakeskins
                    and a dozen books.

The dreams are untrue, too beautiful—
    the black-haired man sings a path
        through mountains now,
            once more you tear
                a cotton dress over your head
                    and find your body clean beneath it.

You rise angry in the dark,
rummage for the knife Jacques gave you.
Twice this new knife has almost
relieved you of your thumb.
You slice away the visions without blinking,
heave them to the cats in the vacant lot,
who are always hungry.

But you lie awake, suspended
in a hammock of shadow and streetlight,
remembering.
Full night long, you listen to the cats
fight and fuck in the skeleton of love,
re-sounding your cries.

You are still listening
when dawn rises from the ground
like a soldier, gray and cold,
afraid of his own power.

The truth is, you were always planning to leave.

The world threw herself open like a laughing woman, like a door made of feathers, like a body of water falling down a thousand fathoms: even the slums of Lisboa and Istanbul heaved like rich oceans. Who could resist such labyrinths, the roads, the street signs with dancing alphabets? The atlas in the study unbound and became an eagle with a snake's tail. It caught you up in its hooked beak.

Now, an ocean distant and a sea away, a sheik from Algeria slaughters a lamb on his kitchen floor. He cooks the best couscous on the European continent. Over mint tea, he swears you have desert eyes. He wants to take you to Africa, his own oasis, he eases your eyelids down with his brown fingers and describes the blue room of echoing walls where you will sleep...

At night, creeks flood your dreams. Paths appear at the edge of the city, trails you know as well as the mare knows them, navigating forever with the star of home on her flanks, between her ears. Half-children curl at the bottom of the pond, lingering in their muddy shells. There are dreams, too, of the man who overthrew you, how you heaved the world upside down to remain standing. God will reward him with warm rooms and diapers. His snapdragons will bloom in December.

The atlas, open, takes you. Who can anchor a heart that longs to be a fish? Thunder, tearing the sheet of sky, takes you. Come, enter this ocean of sharks and shattered light, drink salt and honey by the mouthful. Pay with peace if you have to, but swallow the storm and carry it in your flesh. Why are you afraid to nourish this extravagant desire to devour the world?

Years from now, in a cave in Spain, you will ask a witch if it's greed or a healthy appetite. She will laugh; even her burnished eyes will make a sound like bells. She'll take your face in her hands and whisper, "But, daughter, the world devours you."

The Drowning Stroke

Cities beyond, an abacus
of hours and years reckoned away,
we meet each other again one night

very late, so late.

The whisky and wine alter nothing.
Gold and blood torn from the fruit.
We twist our mouths around small words, quiet
syllables of delight and lost mittens, anecdotes
from New York, phrases from our little towns,
heavy sentences to prove and defend
our present happiness.

You tell me you swam naked
through last summer, you paint
such a clean watercolor,
your wedding ring unsalvageable,
lost among sand
dollars and seaweed.

I remember when you could not drink
enough of me, could not stop swimming
into the deeper, secret basins.

Remember?
You came with me to watch
the slow gorgeous sharks,
their fins slicing the waves
beyond the breakwater.
You came with me.
You admired their immaculate hunger.
Remember?
I showed you
the throb of animals
in the foam, the tide pool.

Recall the rare anemone
pink and blood-pulsed and opening,
flowering for you,
my rose of purple salt and honey,
the flesh round it solid, the lustre
like mother-of-pearl, my splayed legs
hard as polished rock.

Remember that.
Forget it now
in the next breath,
in the drowning stroke
of another year.

I smell rot in your hair, Love.
Time's scarring pulls white
bars down my breasts and hips.
I turn and pace and pivot in my prison
of bone and laughter, a felon
in this flesh you ate
and ate and ate

and fled.

So late, so late.
Can you hear the goblin-ice
gnawing the eyes of the statues?
The ghosts of fish swim black
through the wind on this dying shore.

Don't you know the fishermen here are starving?
Watch their boats list gray and rotten,
bodies swollen with emptiness.
Now do you see them?

Even the vast rocks of this coast
are broken, bones of a giant
who staggered beneath
the frozen weight of stars.

Can't you see them?

And heaving away from the land
we inhabit, as though in fear,
yet still swelling around us
and in our hearts,

behold the squandered sea.

The Disorder of Love

*The best way to know life
is to love many things.*

Vincent Van Gogh

This Woman

Dawn, a bowl of peach light
on the black table of spruce.
The sky yawns into its blueness.
Poplars rub their naked wrists together.
Silence from the earth, enormous and graceful
    as the swooping owl she watched last night.

Like Rembrandt's people breathing out of canvas,
    the horses walk alive from the wakening field,
    push against their frames, the fences.
They stretch out their sleek necks for her.
Even the ugly ones are perfect
    in themselves, strong-backed
    and holy, seraphs whose wings
    have fallen into the water troughs
    and turned into emerald algae.
Jealous ponies chase each other away from her.
Each animal turns slick with spring
as Orion glides under the earth.

Jake steps back into the house and drinks her coffee.
She fills twenty cigarette tubes with tobacco.
The Great Dane groans like a fledgling dragon
and rests his huge head in her lap.
Since her sixth year, she has dreamed
of this belly of peace.
At dawn and dusk she finds it,
in silence and the language of animals.

Her other hours snarl in the city,
in the bowels of a police-station:
    the beaten child wandering the streets of Bowness
    the woman freshly raped, unable to spell her name
    the woman whose husband has locked her in the garage
    the man who finds his son hanging from the rafters

She is intimate with these disasters,
takes the calls with steady hands,
taps in the reports tearlessly.
She declares herself a professional
in the management of human cruelty.
My heart, she says, my poor heart
bangs its head against the walls of the world.

And she coughs her own fairytales, this woman.
Even now, the granddaughter tears up
the city's cliffsides, body scarred
with tire treads and doused in rain.

It's a wet season, she says,
knowing the girl wears sneakers without socks.

In the detention centres, Jake explains,
    the girls play a wicked game.
        They scratch each other until they bleed.
            The winner is the one who does not cry out.
Her granddaughter's arms and hands are striped
with long scabs of endurance.

Jake, my mother,
at the eternal kitchen table of her life,
her love for her children a symphony, a masterpiece
I haven't the guts to fathom yet.

I watch her face alter under the exacting thumbs of time,
that voracious sculptor who molds us into our dying.
The lines around her eyes are nets
heavy with those nights
drowning in the kitchen,
ashes splashed around her hands,
rye and coke by her forearm,
the cigarette sending up relentless signals.
She watched her own mother beaten,
scalp torn and hair matted with blood.

Now she wakes at 5 am,
puts the tobacco away,
and returns to the porch

where morning appears like one more child
sprawled in the grass,
laughing gold in tiger lilies and peonies.

She stands there smiling, this woman

and says, The sweet peas are coming up.
The garden's going to sing this year.

Stray Cat

I know what you saw:
   dawn, the long tawn spill of deer
   through aspen
   the pond a well of clouds
   a dragonfly prying new wings from its old self,
   finished with a childhood of water

I heard what you heard,
filtered through my own flesh:
   the carousing heart
   like a drumming grouse
   or a hammer
   or a fist-beat
      on a guitar's hollow body

See how each thing holds onto the next?
That was the wisdom we were meant to learn
in the woods where we worked and fought
and sucked each other's jealous blood.

Instead we indulged in melodrama and beer,
coyote nights yelping lust,
the music too beautiful for us.
Our backs bowed cold under the stars but our
faces and knees, breasts and feet grew hot
at the firepit.
The flames mocked us for lacking
the courage to shine, to burn,
to acquire a taste for ashes.

Funny we called you Cat
when you were the only innocent
bumbling among hard-mouthed women.
Of course I adored you.
Your scent of lemon and berry
turned the cook house tropical.
We drenched ourselves with insect repellant;
you wore perfume.

I remember your blackened eyes,
despair barely concealed under thin clothes,
those limbs determined to provoke desire
in anyone after Nicolas
picked your breastbone clean
and tossed you away.

But most days, your body forgot
its lithe contours, its woman-spice
and arch and slide.
I am not a great beauty, you said
one afternoon, sighing, but that night
I lay awake wondering why on earth
I hadn't argued with you.

You moved among us for free.
Like a child, you gave away your treasures
in exchange for anything
that sang or smelled or stung like love.

I took nothing from you
and I gave you nothing but
the occasional gin and tonic,
red wine in a jam jar,
those black olives and
tomatoes on the porch.

But I adored you.
Your tigress appetite,
your willow waist.
I could lift you up
    just like that, into wind after rain,
    into my arms, like lifting the muscled
        slimness of a cat

    the stray you finally notice one evening
        and reach for.
You look full into her eyes
    and see the flame enslaved,
        the starving spark inside.

THE QUICK OF HISTORY

We lie on the Abruzzi carpet.
Little else in the living
room except for the desk,
red and blue rice paper prints,
Picasso's dear madman Sebastian,

and paper, scattered
        paper piled
                unsheathed hundreds
                of thin knives

Outside it is snowing.
Every time I live here
it is snowing.
My only life in this city,
the slowest avalanche on earth.

It was my terror as a child
to drown, not in water
but in snow.
They said you didn't know which way was up
or down, you could dig slowly for hours
in the wrong direction, a stupid worm,
freezing to death, crazy
with cold, but you would never
get out, never
escape the heavy white
darkness pressing down, suffocating you
filling your nose eyes mouth ears
all the senses frozen out
gone
        you were trapped
        and no one ever knew.

No one ever knew.

It has been snowing for a long time.

Yet I know I am safe
lying here with you.
One eye brown, one eye blue,
my guileless sorcerer.
Your beard's turning goat-white.
My calloused feet are crossed on your chest.

You pull me closer, taking my hand
to press it down on your torso,
below the ribcage.
    Feel that? you ask, rubbing
my fingers on the hard cords
of gristle under your flesh.
    That's one of the things
    they did to me. Tore open
    the lining of my stomach.

I read the weird Braille of hurt in you,
that scar beneath the skin.
If scars were always visible,
we would be hideous.
Sometimes we're ugly anyway.
Wounds reveal themselves in our voices,
in the way our hands shrink tight
around our assets, in the way
we punish whatever we can.
I know a man who bought a punching bag
and a bible to keep from murdering his father.

The fuckers! you whisper, loudly,
and I howl, Yeah, the fuckers!
Crude agreement is not poetry
but the truth of it is.
Our voices so bare in the bare room.
I am shaking.
We hug each other like two wrestlers
who've suddenly, obscenely, fallen in love.

In this room illumined by winter,
the keen unsentimental light of snow,
we strip history down
until we come to the quick

our raw naked selves
        two children

Then there is only surprise,
a momentary breathless shock:
    we are beautiful.

Desperate For Jazz

I'm a cat born in the age of calamity and famine, and I'm
looking for you. I know I won't find you.
This city is small but not that small. Funny, to be
compelled by idiot hunger. Bloody hilarious, the way lust
drags me out of the house by the hair, sends me stumbling
down the stairs, keys jingling in my hand like jewels stolen
from a drunk, like the bell you wore on your ankle that time,
like your bracelets' jangle when you yank the sweater up
your narrow back, over your head.
Your face, the sly way your eyes enter mine, then swim
away, your hands—masters of puppet jaws and foot massage—
your skin, your exploding laughter, who could resist any of
it? Or the way you smile as your little brown knife glides
under the ripe skin of the mango. "This fruit," you say,
"begs to be eaten."
It is difficult to breathe around you. It is difficult to
speak any comprehensible language.
You push a thick slice of sweet honey-orange into your
mouth, your narrow fingers dripping juice, wet flesh. You
gulp some, you chew more, you say, "There are mango trees
in the yard of the house where I was born."
Am I surprised? Tropical weather precedes you. Petals of
bougainvillea and jasmine fall after you like shreds of silk
lingerie.
Useless to praise this street, the neon emptiness, this
bus-stop bench and traffic snorting toward downtown.
Useless. When was the last time I prowled like this, wishing I
could rip down a rag of the blue night sky and ravage it whole?

The bus stops, the door swings open.

"Sorry, I'm just writing poetry."

The driver smiles. "That's all right." He pulls the door shut with a wink and drives off, trailing exhaust. Oh, the exhaustion of confused lust. To hang upside down from the cliff of desire for a woman who always leaves the party before I do. Who cannot give me her phone number because she has no phone. Who cannot give me her mouth because it is constantly occupied by laughter and slender white cigarettes. I want to eat your cigarettes, Jazz, have I told you? And I don't even smoke.

There's no way to reach you, no way to stretch my hand into your sunlit mornings warm as oranges on the tree. My ass is cold as December marble. You are somewhere in this city but you are not here.

I'm writing this at a bus stop in front of a car-lot on 1st Street. Isn't that pathetic? I'm no longer eighteen, you know, I can't wait until 2 am, I simply won't wait until you walk by...

My feet turn into the cement beneath my shoes. I'm finally feeling tired, writing this, I realize you will not materialize bodily out of one of the brand new Volvos behind me.

You've probably moved anyway, maybe you live on 2nd Street, not 1st, maybe you're in love, maybe you never considered the possibilities beyond foot massage, the skin that extends above the bones of my toes, the soft places past the softness in the centre of the foot, an array of nerves like guitar strings in need of tuning, in need of changing.

Cars, the modern pestilence, bellow and roar by the bus
stop, a man behind every wheel, men with moustaches, men
without, some chiselled Apollos, some in beer shirts and
baseball caps. The cylinders in their engines bore me to death.
    Finally it's so late and cold I can't write anymore. I am
sober and disappointed. My hands are ice-knuckled while
somewhere your body is roasted nutmeg. You smoke a
cigarette with your Trinidad hands, your tropical mouth.
You sip a transparent drink and smile down at the bells of ice.
You contemplate all the people who own phones in this
world, all the women and men who care who calls.
    When you contemplate these people, you lean your head
back, your mouth turns loose its laughter like a red colt.
Hair falls away from your neck a mane, like a night waterfall
dropping silver, like a veil falling down.
    I can see the naked wood of your brown neck.
Wherever you are tonight, I kiss you there.

BURIED AT SEA

"I have small hands, especially
for a sculptor. Very small hands
How can they hold the earth?"

Alexandra Keim

Chocolate almonds on two tongues,
grass beneath four elbows.
Love rises in us like the sap
in these tall spruce.

You have a letter from London.
I have poetry from the coast.
Last night your father quoted Pablo
as we sat in the garden:
Puedo escribir los versos más tristes esta noche...
Es tan corto el amor, y es tan largo el olvido.

But this morning we eat almonds and tell
each other: the gods exist, remember all.
Holiness is here, poetry on the rug,
a dozen books under the lilacs,
marble and glass breathing,
waiting for you in England.

We lounge in our underwear
reading, arguing about mathematics,
the terrifying equations
of distance and love.
When wind heaves the high trees
around us, they sing
about deep water.

I want to be buried at sea,
you tell me.

It's a very complicated procedure.
You have to start years
before the day you die

make arrangements for the cage of mesh,
metal, or plastic, as you prefer.
They bury you in a cage
so your limbs don't float
up to the surface,
so you don't frighten the fishermen from Peru
or ruin a young couple's honeymoon cruise.

Who wants to see an errant skull
bobbing in the moonlight,
the smile flashing fishes
and eye-sockets a dazzle of anenomes?
Who wants to meet a ragged leg
sauntering through the waves?

You want to be buried at sea.
I want to live there.
Yet we have nothing
but this morning
alive on the land.
Our bodies have become mysterious
territory for the ants,
who do not comprehend such polished acres.

You want to be buried at sea,
and a cage must be used
to keep your arms and legs
from swimming back to the sky.

I laugh.
Surely you know your limbs
already float through the world.

Over the mongrel back of this country,
southward, to El Palacio de los Corazones

eastward, through breakers, to England,
where the silver dragon's tail
roared from your fingers

northward, where in St. Petersburg you wove
a wing for a Russian angel

westward, to Gotland, where the Swedish stones
tell riddles of ancient snails
and wolves' teeth bite the tide,
and fish plunge through the cliffs.

Already, you are buried at sea,
you are buried in earth,
even as you rise above me, laughing.

No cage could imprison those hands.

Believe it:
Already your limbs inhabit
the lands, swim the infinite seas.

TARIQ IN THE HOUSE OF
NIGHT BLUES AND TOUCH

I.

Late nights alone in rooms with a ghost,
the blue-eyed woman who dreamed Italy.
The canary in the window box blazes
shreds of fear.
His name is Caruso,
sad fate.
He never sings.

This, a gilded cage of artefacts,
Afghani carpets and tea pots, old photographs
of people I do not know—
yet how their dead eyes arrest me.

Their eyes vault through a century
and land, without a sound, in my throat.

II.

The ghost of this English house
was born in China.
You were born in Pakistan.
I was born down the street.
Yet we meet here, between the faces
of gracious paintings, our hands around
glasses of gin.
We feel the ice on our hot palms.
We smile.

Yours, the teeth of a king.
Your fingers jointed at the ends
like a Balinese dancer's,
though you explain you are a musician.
We will work together this summer.
You will teach me something about music.

III.

Hands are strange animals,
shape-shifters.
This year my hands are tough, solitary spiders.
My shoulders shrug into and out of sweaters
carelessly, I drink the river
with my own throat, alone.
Silence its own music
in a house like this
where symphonies and string
quartets were poured with the foundation,
hammered into the walls, planted with the roses.
Puccini and Verdi compose in each room.

I would like to have commerce with this house
every day, stay inside and breathe
her history as you breathe
a lover's sleep, collecting the eyelids'
tremor like gold dust.

But my days have been bought
by the Alberta government.
I have sold my days: I am damned.
The office slumps like a warty monster
in the foreground of this poem.

Squint. You will see it. It looms
all around you.

IV.

8:15 am
I've already been driving for an hour.
I'm at work behind a metal desk, actively
slaughtering my children.
I crush ten thousand words
like delicate eggs under my own thumbs.
My shape-shifting hands are mallets now,
my hands are murderous bricks.

Friends ask why I sound so foreign
here, in the country of my birth.

When the paycheque witch approaches,
    bearing apples and ribbons,
    combs for my hair,
        poetry squawks away in terror.
Poetry is a bird of paradise
wise to poachers.

If you give your life,
they'll give you a dishwasher,
a Rabbit, a suburban graveyard
to bury it in.

They'll give you all this, and more,
much more, and you will applaud as you watch them
pull the fingers off your soul.
Later, you will experience relief, calm.
Like having a lobotomy but tidier.
No sponges, no scalpels, no visible scars.

V.

You say that if you had lived in Pakistan,
you would not be a musician.
But I think you're wrong.
Even now, the twin you never met is there,
pivoting in the street's river,
its women and men themselves a strain of music.
Your brother stands on the bank of a million lives
in a road splashed with rain and dogs,
the bronze curtain of his body open.

These echoes are inescapable.
These echoes make us
as living sound makes them.
I know this from the old house,
the blue-eyed ghost.

VI.

So much for Greek islands
and swimming naked over
obsidian sand.
It rains every day in July.
The only sunlight in this jungle
filters through your mouth.
All the women's magazines say

DON'T GET INVOLVED WITH A CO-WORKER

so I do it, quickly, quickly as possible.
At least you're not married.
The progress of age.

Still, I understand the great love affair
this summer is between you
and your new guitar.

Look at those curves, you say,
the ideal woman, café-au-lait body,
cello-heart, hooves of Arabian rhythm.

Now, night blues and touch

    fingers curved around the pale neck
    of the guitar in your arms.

Caruso
the terrified canary,
did not sing
until you came,
played here.

VII.

Slowly. Slowly.
See the vines crave
the broken wall.
Up, up. Down, deeper
through the crevice,
over the edge, into
the garden.

Goldfish light darts in, out of your mouth.
Red leaves grow and fall down the paintings.
An English house, but you bring me to India
beneath the shawl of your body.

Shadows tiger-stripe the table,
the chairs, the walls, the bed.
Your shadow yet another ghost,
such rich black smoke, the cardamon
crushed in the mortar and pestle
of our hip bones and hollows, the cilantro
green on our lips, sandalwood sweat
down the neck.

We oil the cinnamon,
set it aflame like a candle
to cast light,
to ignite
our selves.

THE BODY SUDDENLY

The body suddenly
exotic, slick, rising from the desert
like a creature we've never seen before,
    a beast we could not have borne,

        not us, with our hearts dipped in tar,
        tossed on the rocks.

Fledglings born in a parched country,
we licked the salt that ices life,
licked and sucked, insatiable for spoil.

The caves we lived in smelled
of old blood, bitten tongues.
We kept our treasures buried under
a blanket of sand and lies.
I did not know you then
but at night I prayed
for an animal like myself,
any woman who coveted silver
and sunlight, the ruthless glint
of the real.

Common guilt gifted us with each other.
Ours the sin of shining in a gray country.

*   *

Your body suddenly
broken into light, pried open
in the dark, a pomegranate
of blood and flowers.

I dip my hands into the river
of you, the long sweet waters
of your body

and the desert draws back,

the desert dies.

Tomorrow you will be in Africa

For Sandra and David,
talisman and prayer,
a poem for your journey

Black dogs barking in the snow.
Midnight in the back alley, white
holding down every sound
just a moment longer.
The candleflame is not high enough tonight.

Tomorrow you will be in Africa,
and I am crying.

*

With you gone,
what can I love?

*

With you gone,
how will I laugh?

How will I escape the beast
that stalks the city, the giant
shopping mall we all fear?
Franchise food slides into franchised bodies.
Ah, the grease of complicity!

Construction sites in the piggish suburbs:
the fresh-dug basements are very large
open-mouthed graves, big enough
for entire dysfunctional families,
fully-equipped rec rooms, two metre television screens,
personal computers, hundreds of plastic
and nylon sex toys.

*

You are a raging bull
with two Leicas around your neck.
All the idiot world's wearing red.
Fury aside, your laughter is God's own
personal joke, contagious,
a holy plague.

And you are the delicate
twelve-year-old with blue lights
in your face; eyes that shine open
the shuttered world.

Always between us, beneath us,
words, words like a raft
of half-rotted timbers.

Listen, you told me,
trying to convince yourself,

> This raft will be enough
> > we will learn to navigate by the stars
> > we will study the winds
> > we will remember the ways of salt and blood
> This raft will take us home.

*

Oh, Africa.
I am too small.
How can I know your greatness?

They have promised me your paper-thorns
and a tiger's eye.
They will send faces from the land,
a deep poem about your sky,
an envelope coated, inside,
with sienna dust.

Africa,
from this winter,
with all my ignorance,
I ask you:

Please, take care of them.

PANDORA STREET, LATE NOVEMBER

with apologies to Kevin Paul

When I woke up
it was raining
and she was gone.
The window was open
to the silver
eyes of the world.
My shoulders were cold.

The sound of horses' hooves
clapping the road outside
made me think
I was in another country

but I wasn't.
I was in this country,
land of my body,
naked and alone.
I heard rain falling
off the roof.
I could not hear
the ocean.

On the desk
the driftwood we had gathered
the day before, two mottled stones
like petrified eggs,

and her note, written on hotel stationery,
a short treatise on the inadequacy
of my hands, the failure
of vagabond lust

(each word self-conscious,
innocently vengeful,
each word aware
it was not a wave,
not a wind,
not her warm mouth):

    You still don't know
    anything
    about me.

ALEXANDRA

She lay upstairs
inhaling the night,
asleep, her hair unbound on the pillows.
Mouth open slightly, her face
grave and beautiful, engaged
in the fervent waltz of sleep.
Both arms flung open over the burgundy quilt.
She was dancing motionless like that
when I left her
and came down in the dark
to watch the moon, white,
rove over the whiter hills.
I thought of nothing but
her breasts,
my mouth.

I sat crying in front
of the big window, filled
with the inchoate emptiness
of moon-sky and snow.
I was feeling the surprise of it,
the absurdity, even,
and the absolute rightness
of such a landscape.
The way her ivory back was
like my own but smaller,
a smooth plain of
heat, strength, the long
hunger that leads eventually
to the mouth,
to the cunt.

I had never seen so much
clean white turned platinum,
rose-purple, blue in the dark.

I sat in the silent house.
For awhile, coyotes.
Once, her cough,
which made me still and hopeful
because it had the raw silk
of her voice in it.
I wanted her to call my name,
but she slept on
turning slowly in her dance,
tangled in tassels of dream
and breath, quiet

because I had loved her
well enough.

She has no idea
how awake I am,
after such long sleep:
it doesn't matter.
This is the way things
are now, these hills,
my life filled with
depths, roundnesses,
the deep basins of the land
she lives in,
the land she is.

MONTREAL

We are back again in winter.
As lovers we leave behind the blankets
    and face the real mirror,
        the glimmering imprisonment of hands, our faces,
            all the world's nakedness
                in these two bodies.

Two mornings in Montreal.
Even this ashen light reveals too much.
Another day in another apartment.
A bed on the floor.
Someone else's sheets
    and then the difficult mystery of
        who has slept here and
            what colour was her hair

One wine-coloured earring
on the piano

water glass, old water

another dirty window pane
    avalanche of concrete outside
        a small man floundering in the snow
            the alley like a frozen tongue

(though even now, we know,
a building burns in this city,
black icicles hang from
flame-shattered windows)

What I have loved always
    is the way your body insists
        on summer, the drum
            pounding *inside* your fingers.

81

What I have loved always
    are your hands, your
        voice the source
            of summer, those hours,
                tons of light firing
                    the mountain rivers.

Tons of snow flood
    the streets of Montreal.
Another radiator
    inhabited by nails
        and water snakes.
Another telephone ringing,
        ringing, a voice from
            a separate star singing
                your name.

This has nothing to do
    with betrayal
        and everything to do
            with different time zones.

I break my neck
    tripping over clouds
    and continents.
You sit naked
    at the out-of-tune piano
    playing anyway.

You are a map gently torn
    with folding and refolding.
I am chaos in a dress, dragging
    a suitcase of wind and shells.

What I have loved always
    are your hands
            that hold the birds of summer
    and let them go
    let them go all at once

        singing

Evidence of God

The colour of Canadian rye whisky
is not really the colour of amber
or liquid gold
but more the colour of my mother's voice
when she is drunk,
too warm, embarrassing,
an out-of-tune guitar played in minors
so you know the player is dishonest,
not to be trusted, dangerous
as only the deeply sentimental can be,
because they dread
the sandpaper hands
of the truth.

Not to say my mother is dangerous
but of course she is, we all are
when we hurt those who love us
when our own pain overshadows
the blessings and reminds us
of nothing but our pain,
our own pain, our own pain.
It's a boring litany, but popular,
difficult to unlearn, difficult
to forget, as the lines to bad songs
always are.

I can't blame her really,
but sometimes I do.
It wasn't so bad anyway,
though it was, and the badness
lives on and on, I can't kill it.
It's like one of those deathless Chinese demons
I've been reading about.
All demons are deathless,
unlike sisters and brothers.
Demons are the colour
of Canadian rye whisky
and weeping, the colour of
the turquoise scarf
my brother stole years ago
and sold.

He is selling again, not scarves,
drugs, though I believed for a time
he was home, in his senses.
When we talk now, it is once again
through fog, the ungraspable cape of a demon.
When he speaks I cannot hear
his voice, I hear the little asshole
gargoyle gnawing his heart.
My brother doesn't understand.
He opened his mouth and begged the demon in.
Of the body, I love the hands most,
but I see my family is a family of mouths,
of openings and closings, ingestations,
vomit, grunts, and howls.
Hands naked remind me of tree branches,
mouths remind me of graves, isn't that strange?

But that's what I see, my brother
breathing demons, my mother
drinking them, my father owned
by them now, hung in their barren realm
like a scarecrow on a stake, still blinking.
My sister ate demons and ate them
and finally choked to death on their bones.

And, I, too, am a creature of the mouth, the tongue.
But I am a lucky one, I learned the difficult
and late-night art of singing demons
out of me, out of my body, away
into the wind
or onto paper

where they are
no longer demons

but gifts.

CHAOS IS A GREEK WORD

walk here girl
where everything
answers your nakedness

Kenneth White

FRAGMENTS

What fills a day?
Grace and poison,
the body of a snake.

The almond shell
cradles the tree.

Dusk, when dust comes
gold and certain stones
the colour of his hands,
full of blood, signed
by scars.

Only the white horse
is saved from the black
swallow falling, night.

Candle in the dark.
Come the moth, the praying
mantis with agile hands.
How she plucks the red beetles,
like rosebuds, from the breeze.

Splendid minnows, the meteors,
shoot from deep space
into the shallows of the sea.

A man walks away.
In his arms he carries
thick swathes of oregano.
A hundred bees follow him
singing like children.

When he whistles
absentmindedly
a naked woman wakes
in a stone house.

At dawn, a red scorpion walks
slowly across her notebook, beyond
her words.

Goat's horn,
truth that grows like stone.
Spun-gold eyes.
The white song of milk.

Bent back, a drum beaten by sunlight.
Every rib a xylophone key.
The world plays me.
A breeze in the windpipe,
wind held by the silver fingers
of the olive trees.

Every garden bends the knees.
The men of this island pray
long hours in the sun.

Promise you will return.
Return and touch
the sea-tamed stones.
Return and stand here
with naked feet.

Give your eyes
to the water.
Offer your one life
to this last blue
altar of sky.

YIORGOS AND SHIPAKE

Kitten-surge out of the wooden wheelbarrow,
green and scarlet garden-splash up the fence.
Yiorgos rides in, horse caravan
jingling bells, saddle-tools, trunks
bulging leather, silver-spilling pouches.
Wilderness of white hair overruns his head.
He plants a garden across the road,
hangs a bed in the biggest olive tree.
I meet him at the water-tap in the road.
I have curiosity for you, he says.

Mornings we slurp thick coffee,
see distant ships drop off the horizon.
I watch him dance with his horses.

This spring the bay colt
sheds his coltishness and bucks
at the touch of a saddle.
He spends hours whetting his hooves
on the stony cliffs above the sea.
Finally, wind charging towards afternoon,
he breaks from the mare
with his first real scream,
a savage toss of mane and muscle.

Tethered, she tries calling him back,
but he gallops hard for the gate, through it
and down, pounding the hillside, towards Maria
and her terrified sheep.
He's weaned himself, Yiorgos laughs,
the mare has lost him.

But the vision still turns, flickers
in each burning eye, in every muscle.
Down the long bones of the jaw,
memory lopes, dreaming,
of the mother.

Panselinos

We stumble down the mountain, whipped
with sun, drowned by the blue
giant heaving below us.
We whisper to each other once, again,
like an encantation,
    Almond blossoms smell like honey.

It's spring, it's coming tonight,
the full moon of April, newborn lamb
still round and sleek in the sky.

Late dusk, we're hungry, we haven't eaten
since dawn, we watch the backbone of the cliff
arch over night's arms, we see night's mouth
devour the day. You turn, look at me
and say, I'm starving.

We walk to the village square
where children dance in awe under the lamps,
watching the halo of moths grow and burn.
Each of us a witness to light
bred by darkness.

We live under the sun, but it's the moon we worship, *la luna*,
the moon, *to fengari*, the mysterious lover,
she's coming out tonight, complete, *panselinos*,
completely naked, while we sit here swallowing oysters,
watching her shoulders shimmer below the hills.

Impossible opal, glowing round bone.
I cannot believe there are footprints on her body.
I do not believe men know what she's made of.

We're waiting for her, you and I,
drawing the violin bow of this wine
over and down our tongues.

Her back clears the mountains now, slowly,
she floats like a jewel high above our hands.
We cannot name the orchard of stars
but we know the moon, *panselinos*, April, she floods
the sky with an original sea, spills silver
in the Aegean, heaves a tide of unearthly blue
above us, a shade my words fail to conjure,
    the indigo heart of a seahorse,
    Athena's irises after love.

The moon is a pearl made for the palm of a goddess,
la luna is a pool of milk.
Somewhere in the village, a woman wakes
to nurse her youngest son.
She stands at the open window,
hair glowing with the dark.
She smiles when the child reaches
open-mouthed to the window, thirsty,
his small hands stretching for the moon.

THE RUBY-GROWING STONE

On this island of sheep and spiders, lost hedgehogs,
I discover a starving dog and her three naked saviours,
giggling savages in the sun.
We're learning Greek. We live here now, they say,
tossing me their snorkel.

The oldest boy is Adam.
His body was blessed at birth by a dolphin.
He shows me how to follow the green fish
with purple fins.
We play tag in underwater Byzantium,
push and drift through palaces of rays and urchins and eels.
In slow-motion blue, he waltzes me around pillars
    of sunlight, proving the sea
    and nothing else holds up the horizon.
Adam does not fall but dives down grinning,
    returns with a handful of sand
    to show he's touched the rippled belly of the Aegean.

Later, on the beach, the youngest boy reveals
a perfect red pebble in his wet palm.
This is a ruby-growing stone, he declares.
Ah, six-year-old wisdom, my master of tornadoes
and Oz, owner of Dorothy's red shoes:
    How can I doubt you?

The land of passionate deities imparts a simple prayer:
Please allow me this.

These trees and flowers, a thousand monstrous beauties
    of red wasp and black beetle,
        each bat diving under a lake of stars,
    all the living stones:
        charms in this garden.
Every road of rock and dust a path
through this garden.

While the moon's silver tongue licks salt from the sea,
    the children show me rose quartz and old coins,
        jelly-fish and dinosaur eggs.
Under that field of mint, they explain, *is an ancient cemetery.*
Dead B.C. people live there, affirms the boy
    with the magic shoes.

Eyes wide, he whispers, *That's how we got here.*
    I just said There's no place like home
            There's no place like home,
                then tapped my red heels together.
                    When we opened our eyes, we were here!

When I laugh, he becomes angry.
Really, he insists, *it's true.*

Suddenly I see he's not joking.
It is true, for those welcomed by these shores.
When we open our eyes, we are right *here*,
eating cucumbers and feta on Sappho's sand,
sienna-naked, in mad love with the day.

Antigone

Antigone at dusk,
her back to Sympathy.
A woman in a white shirt
sitting in the sand.
It is impossible for you
to know her now, though you
recall the legend of her name.

Darkness slowly fills the air
with purple sand.
Departure.
Her eyes launch into the Aegean.
Her hair is like a black mare's mane.
The entire sea gradually becomes
the colour of this hair.
Antigone.
You call out to her, perhaps,
but she does not recognize your voice.
She does not recognize the beauty
of her own face.

The poem of a body in darkness
is written in Braille.
Only fingers can know the words.

Antigone is gone,
though her shirt still glows
white like a sail.
She might be arriving now
in a new country.
She sits in the sand,
salt dried on her hands
like bone-dust.

You can hear the voices
of small children
playing around her
like lunar moths
around a cold star.

LATE AUGUST ON LESVOS

Late August on Lesvos, the garden thickens with seed.
A Babylon of butterflies seduces the flowers.
Dawn and dusk, nectar rises in saffron tides.
Even the sea shines like a giant's bowl of honey.

Yiorgos and I live in a chaos of watermelons.
Mikhaili heaves the green treasures to his pigs.
Panagos rolls them under every bench and bed in the house.
Goats trip over them and donkeys sink
grateful teeth into the cool rinds.

Black seeds root in our bellies, send tendrils
of jewel up our spines.
Our dreams are vines winding us
into the astonishing red halls of dawn.

August, yes, I sleep outside and wake at five
to fourteen goddesses setting the stage of the world.
They paint the backdrop of this extravagant theatre
shades of ruby and violet, a flawless set, silhouette
of stone house and fence and grape vine
sprawling black against the sky.

Beyond the road, fig trees stretch awkward white arms
above mauve thistles, yellow thorns.
A thousand years later, the desert souls
are still humbled by their fruit:
        green sea anemones hide crimson tentacles of sugar.

August on the island, before I open my eyes
I hear the kittens purring, feel the white dog curled
in the crook of my knees, her fur a miracle of new snow.
Sometimes the black goat escapes and wakes me herself,
two cleft hooves knocking on my chest,
velvet nose at my ear.

Feast of late summer, the sun exhausts the gardens,
the valley is an upturned table, spilling,
spilling, tomatoes like edible rubies,
almonds splashing into the water basin,
stars falling from the sky like fruit.

Deep August on the island, the dazzling blade of days
pares the moon down until it hangs beyond us
like one bloodied fang of the tigress.

Always the light speaks first,
light, who writes her own chant in passing,
the way brilliance deepens as it fades.

The first day of September is still summer,
old women say, but the heat stands up
like a lover denied and walks away
so slowly, glancing back,
back down the path, pulling fistfuls
of leaves from the trees.

The gardens fill with amber-red sugar,
    tangles of goat-skin in the dust,
    baskets barren but dripping dusk.

Still summer, the old shepherd says,
waving wrinkled hands through kindled air,
but what do we see in the skeleton-vines
and the footprints haunted by ants?

What do we finally harvest from gardens
but the gold weight of death,
that heavy fruit,
its frightening grace.

The September Letter

Among mouse droppings, dust in the urgent papers,
I find your last letter, tales of children and garlic
and spring gliding into your valley
like a woman flying down a slide.

I don't know if you've written since then.
Chaos is a Greek word:
    Athenian politics have poisoned the mailman,
    strikes all summer long, no signs
    from my cold-rock country.
The cities sink into memory's sediment, wide streets awash
with red and yellow leaves, first ice-water
wind of autumn splashing the neck.
The people there grow a fleece of dust.

Your last letter.
Grit envelopes the paper now, sepia
seeps in from the sun-curled edges.
I've circled the date, *May 7, late evening*

but this morning, September swallows her tail
like a famished snake, the hot scales
of summer disappear and a chill wind
rides in, prophesying winter.
The ants' desperation is contagious.
They rush in a hunt for the edible,
tracking earth, ankles, walls, drowning
in the marmelade and milk pails, licking
the essence out of walnut shells.
How do those tiny slaves
own such mammoth hunger?

Have the ants in your garden already gone underground?
It's colder there, frost and gloves in the morning.
Let me remember where you live.
Where you live
hold that phrase in the mouth,
taste its small but supreme weight,
a bloodstone on the tongue.

I know you wake up early.
Jam sweetens your fingers, children's voices
rise, plunge like swallows, so quickly,
perpetual bearers of sunlight.

Where are the windows
in that house I've never seen?
I didn't live in houses this year.
I existed on trains.
Even the rooms I slept in
were abandoned compartments
whose close walls whispered,
Do not rest here, do not stay.

Cities close to borders claimed my life
until I came to the island,
took the sea as my frontier and washed
Baudelaire's acidic verses from my eyes.
Finally this exile teaches me
to seek the greeting, not the escape,
of the roads beneath my feet.

I've dreamt my body as a storm,
but this season the calm rolls closer,
from the east.

Have I found a place to rest?
Across the water the hills of Turkey
shimmer and sway like a purple caravan.

You can't quite see it, can you?
No, nor these hills carved from the gold
and olive-green thigh-bones of God.
My words will never hold
the winds and light of these hours.
I don't know what to do
with the grace here, where to offer
my prayers when the temples stand in ruins.

I want to give you this place
like the exotic fruit we were denied
as children, press it deeply
into your palm and whisper,
        Taste this, Eve's sin,
                eat the same ripe glory.

I'm returning soon, to stay
until your children know my voice again.
Figs dried under this sun are yours,
a sac of almonds, this cologne
of goats and ouzo.

I will smash a glass, offer you a Turkish cigarette.
We'll lean together while the windows
deepen like cold wells, reflect faces
drowning in the swell of night and time.

But even this will not still our hands,
our voices praising
the miracles of the age.

VOULA

Rebetiko is a hypnotic, passionate style of music and dance which became popular in Greece in the 1930's and '40's. It was, and still is, the music of the poor and of social outcasts, similar in many ways to Gypsy Flamenco. Traditionally it is played and danced only by men.

Little spot

is the meaning of my name,
but look at me, my life
is big as the sun, I am Voula,
I am famous.

"She is ugly," they'll tell you,
"a dirty-dog woman, a junkie
covered in sores
and a bitch besides,"

but look at my young lovers,
texna-mou,
Sonia from Brazil,
Katerina from the north,
Sinead from Ireland with
all her silk and lace.

I am Voula
I am famous.

If you see me dance *rebetiko*
you too will love me,
you will watch and look away
with burning eyes.
Even Vaso's plates know
the disorder of love, they leap
off the tables and shatter
just to touch my feet.

With these scuffed boots
I sway hard and slow inside
the music, my arms in the air,
elbows crooked above my head:
I am balancing each star high
above the plane trees.

I close my eyes to dance like this.
You have to close your eyes
to see inside music,
to see inside a woman,
and to see inside the gods.

The accordian and I
breathe the warm night wind.
The mandolin has my curves,
the same thin hardness and dirty
fingerprints all over her body.

Sweat shines like oil on my forehead.
I dance so slowly, a snake
without legs, without arms,
held up by the taut nerves
of music.

I have given my limbs to you.
I have given my eyes to you.
I am naked in my dance,
in this night
under the plane trees.

Na zeis helia kronia!
Na zeis panda!

May you live a thousand years.
May you live forever.